# ★ ★ ★ TABLE OF CONTENTS ★ ★ ★

**INTRODUCTION ★ PRINCIPLES OF SUCCESS** *3*

**STEP 1 ★ STUDY SMART** *4*

**STEP 2 ★ HAVE A GREAT SHOWREEL** *6*

> In « Step 2 », this guide will provide you with an overview of the Film Industry players : what you need to know and who you should focus on knowing in order to become a succesful actor(ess).

**STEP 3 ★ NETWORK** *8*

**STEP 4 ★ FIND A TALENT AGENT** *10*

**REVIEW ★ THE 15 GOLDEN RULES** *13*

> The last page of this handbook is a Review of the 15 Rules you need to follow and read everyday.

**ANNEX ★ YOUR PERSONALIZED DAILY ACTION PLAN** *15*

> The Annex of this handbook is a daily checklist of what you have to do. Just fill it out everyday. Do it for 30 days. Just do it. You will be amazed of the results in only 30 days. Then, it will become a habit until you are a successful actor(ess).

©2010, Marc Gordon

# PRINCIPLES OF SUCCESS

SOME PEOPLE HAVE DONE IT. THIS ONLY MEANS THAT IT IS POSSIBLE.
SO, WHY NOT YOU?
YOU CAN DO ANYTHING.
YOU AND ONLY YOU CONTROL YOUR DESTINY.

When Leonardo di Caprio, Brad Pitt, Matt Damon or Cameron Diaz told their parents and friends that they wanted to become the most succesful actor(ess) or of the 2Oth century, do you think that their parents told them : «sure honey, go for it.That will happen.» ?
Probably not. They most surely were worried like most parents.
Or jealous in some way, like most friends who don't have the courage to do what it takes to follow and achieve their dream.

**Trust yourself. Trust your dream.**
Don't listen to anybody. Most of people will try to discourage you.
Basically, your life is like the lottery: only winners have played. Successful people have at least tried to achieve their dream at a moment or another. Pure luck does not exist.
We have only one life. So it is up to you to follow and live your dream.
**Just do it. But do it smartly.**

The basic principle of success is to put all the chances on your side in order to achieve your dream. It is purely mathematical. It is the matter of probabilities.

In order to become a successful actor:

Of course, you need to have talent and work on your acting.
Of course, good looks and charisma help. Taking care of yourself, exercising, is crucial.
Of course, if your native tongue is not English: speaking English, ideally without any accent, is compulsory.
That's the basis.

**BUT THE PRIMARY OBJECTIVE IS TO GET EXPOSURE:
TO FIND A TALENT AGENT.**

©2010, Marc Gordon

The talent agent will give you access to auditions, hence acting jobs.
Getting representation from a prestigious and efficient talent agent is the most difficult part.
This handbook will assist you in putting all the chances on your side in order to find one.
Then, see you at the Academy Awards !

**YOUR ACTION PLAN NEEDS TO FOLLOW THE FOLLOWING STEPS:**

STEP 1 ★ Study smart

STEP 2 ★ Have a great showreel

STEP 3 ★ Network

STEP 4 ★ Find a talent agent

★

# STEP 1 ★ STUDY SMART

You need to go study and work on your acting skills in an acting school that will:

(1) improve your acting ; and
(2) be a source of invaluable information and resources ; and
(3) help you build a lifetime network for your career and give you access to concrete acting opportunities.

★ **Where to study?**

YOU HAVE TO BE WHERE IT HAPPENS: THE SCHOOL TO BE.

Location is fundamental.
Would you go study Fashion in Missouri?
Hopefully NO, you would go to New York, Paris or Milan.
It is true that anything can happen. Luck exists, pure luck does not. Someone can notice you walking in a supermarket but it is unlikely. Again, it is only a matter of probabilities. So, why be dumb about it?
It is best to put all the chances on your side.

<u>**Conclusion:**</u>
**It is much better to go study acting in New York or Los Angeles, where the Film Industry is.**
Where you will build your network everyday.
Then, it is up to you to make it happen.

Please find below a short list of the most serious and connected schools in New York City and L.A.. The choice of your school is fundamental as it will be your first platform of networking. If your are foreign, please note that these schools will provide you with a student visa.

**In New York City:**

The Lee Strasberg Institute
115 East 15th Street
New York, NY 10003-2188
Phone: (212) 533-5500
www.strasberg.com

The New York Film Academy
100 E. 17th Street
New York, NY 10003
Phone: (212) 674-4300
www.nyfa.com

NYU Tisch School of Arts
721 Broadway street
New York, NY 10003
Phone: (212) 998 1800
www.tisch.nyu.edu

The Actors Studio
432 West 44th Street
New York, New York 10036
Phone: 212-757-0870
www.theactorsstudio.org

**In Los Angeles:**

The Beverly Hills Playhouse
254 S. Robertson Blvd.
Beverly Hills, CA 90211
Phone: (310) 855-1556
www.bhplayhouse.com

The Lee Strasberg Institute
7936 Santa Monica Boulevard
West Hollywood, CA 90046
Phone: (323) 650-7777
www.strasberg.com

The Sanford Meisner Center
5124 Lankershim Boulevard
North Hollywood, CA 91601-3717
Phone: (818) 509-9651
www.themeisnercenter.com

* Again, if you are foreign, you need to have a perfect American accent.
Acting is horribly competitive. You will compete with thousands of young native American actors/(esses) so you need to be at the same level of English than them in order to compete at the same level.
Otherwise, build your acting career in your home country first and then go to the U.S.A.: talent agents are always looking for the next star. If you happen to have a role in a foreign film that will be of international critical acclaim (by being selected or winning a film festival such as Berlin, Cannes, Toronto, Venice or Sundance), talent agents will call you directly to meet with you. They will fight to sign you.

Otherwise, the best way to correct your accent is to get a coach or to take classes of « Reduction of Accent ». It is worth the investment.
Ask your acting shool who they would recommend as a coach.

★

# STEP 2 ★ HAVE A GREAT SHOWREEL

**Your objective is to find a talent agent who will represent you and give you access to auditions.**

★ **Why a talent agent would represent you?**

Because the talent agent believes that you could be the star of tomorrow. And get his 10% commission on your paycheck.
Finding a talent agent is like finding a job: you need to apply and convince them that you are worth their time and investment.
In order to find a job, you send a resume.
In order to find a talent agent, you show a reel of your acting.
If you have the chance to meet a talent agent, the first thing the agent will ask you is : « Show me your reel ». If you don't have a showreel handily ready, he will say : « Come back when your reel is ready ».
Without a showreel, you can't get a serious talent agent to represent you.
So first, build your showreel.
This will be your business card. Your passport to success and fame.

A showreel is a DVD that compiles (1) your resume, (2) pictures of yourself and (3) scenes in which you have acted.

<u>**Conclusion:**</u> **You need to act as much as possible and get your acting filmed.**

**If you are an acting school student:**

1- Write your resume: ask your acting school, teacher(s), to show you some samples of working actors' resumes;

2- Ask your acting school, teacher(s), to show you some samples of working actors' showreels, ask them as well who can actually execute for you the showreel;

3- Have someone filming you during classes;

©2010, Marc Gordon

4- Try to get some acting jobs/scenes in independent films. Go to NYU and the NY Film Academy. Aspiring writers/directors always seek actors in order to shoot their first short film or feature. See below « STEP 3 ★ Network ».

5- Check out Myspace and Youtube to watch actors' pages and videos. Get inspired on how you would like to present yourself.

6- Create your own page on Myspace, Facebook and Twitter. Post videos on these websites. This is a great alternative to practice your acting and have a talent agent notice you.

7- Modelling experience may help (1) to get beautiful pictures of yourself (2) to network. See below « STEP 3 ★ Network ».

**If you are already a working actor, include in your showreel:**

1- Your resume and pictures.

2- The best scenes of the films, TV series, TV shows, in which you have played. The more diverse acting experiences you can show, the more versatile actor you demonstrate to be.

★

# STEP 3 ★ Network

## ★ KNOW THE MARKET - INDUSTRY PLAYERS

### -TALENT AGENT:

Agent working for a talent agency: CAA (Creative Artists Agency), WME (William Morris Endeavor), ICM (International Creative Management), UTA (United Talent Agency) and The Gersch Agency are the most significant ones.

They represent talent: actors, writers, directors, below the line crew and often producers. A talent agent's primary role is to procure you acting jobs and negotiate your contracts. Talent agencies are at the epicenter of the Industry as they centralize all information about films to be produced, whether independent films or studio films. Once a talent agent has signed you, his role is to « sell » you to independent producers and studios. He will give you access to auditions and fight for you and your work to get you an acting job.

A talent agent usually commissions 10% of your future paychecks.
NEVER PAY AN AGENT UPFRONT. Him asking you to pay him upfront only shows that he is not serious about actually finding you acting jobs. Otherwise, he would be confident that he can obtain you jobs, hence being paid on your future paychecks.

### - CASTING DIRECTOR:

A casting director does not represent any clients. A casting director (and/or casting assistant, casting associate) is hired by a studio or an independent production company to recruit actors and extras during pre-production of a particular film. In addition the "CD" may also remain as liaison between director, actors and their agents once the parts have been cast.

Most famous casting directors are Mary Jo Slater, Mary Selway, Lynn Stalmaster, Tammara Billik, Mindy Marin, Marci Liroff, and Vinnie Potestivo. The significant organization of professional screen and theater casting in the US is the Casting Society of America (CSA).

Casting directors usually contact talent agent with the description of the part and the type of actor(ess) they are looking for in order to find the right actor(s) for the film they have been hired to cast.

### - MANAGER:

Unlike agents, managers are not required to be licensed by a US State to practice. They also are free to take as high a commission as their clients are willing to pay. Their commission is usually 20%.

The manager's role is to provide day-to-day and long-term career advice for actors. They have fewer clients than a typical talent agent and focus more on advising him rather than actually find jobs for him.

At this stage of your career, you need to focus on finding a talent agent who will find you jobs. You will seek a manager later on: when you are set as a new rising star and you need more specific advice on how to build your career and reach the top of the Hollywood star system.

### - PRODUCER:

A Producer is the one who manufactures a film. He usually originates or recognizes the next « great idea » for a film and put together all the creative and financial elements in order to actually « produce » such a film. He can be compared to a chief of orchestra.

### - PUBLICIST:

A publicist is a person whose job is to generate and manage publicity for a celebrity. Unlike agents or managers, publicists typically take a monthly fee for serving a client. One of the publicist's main functions is to generate press coverage on behalf of clients and to serve as the bridge between clients, their public and media outlets. A publicist writes press releases, manages campaigns and performs other public relations functions.

### ★ NETWORK

Your 2 objectives are:
1. Find a talent agent
2. Get some acting jobs

These two objectives are intertwined:

In order to find acting jobs, you need an agent.

In order to find an agent, you need to show him some acting.

**Conclusion: network as much as possible in order to (1) get some acting jobs and (2) find a talent agent.**

### 1- ACT, ACT, ACT

- Again, **use your acting school**: ask your teacher(s) if they know anyone seeking actors for theatre, student or independent films, TV shows.

- Check out independent films (« indie » films) at the NY Film Academy, NYU Film School, etc… in order to meet upcoming writers and directors.

- Modelling experiences may help to get exposure.

- Find open calls for auditions for films and TV shows.

- Question to ask whenever you meet with young actors, writers, directors, students, teachers etc… whether at school, through friends or even while partying:

« Are you aware of any student film, Indie film, TV show, theatre play where I could have a small part? »

## 2-NETWORK

1- Make a list besides CAA, ICM, WME, UTA and The Gersch Agency of agents to be targeted: « **The List** ».

Do your research: get a membership on « www.Imdbpro.com » and look up new young upcoming actor who you believe are on the verge of becoming stars:

WHO REPRESENTS HIM/HER? AND COMPLETE THE LIST.

**Exemple:**
Who represented Robert Pattinson prior to « Twilight »? Zac Efron? Nathalie Portman?

2- Question to ask whenever you meet with young actors, writers, directors, students, teachers etc…:

« Do you know any talent agent OR casting director OR manager OR anybody (directors, producers, lawyers, actors, friends, managers, publicists) I could meet with for career advice? Do you have an agent? Who is he/she? »

**And complete your List.**


## CONCLUSION OF STEP 3

**EACH TIME YOU MEET WITH SOMEONE IN THE INDUSTRY:**

1- Get his/her business card;

2- Be polite: be thankful for their time. If you are polite with them, they will be more willing to introduce you to other people as they know you will behave in an a considerate way.
Always write a follow-up email saying for exemple:
« Dear (Name),

©2010, Marc Gordon

It was really nice meeting you. Thank you very much for your time and consideration. Your advice is invaluable to me. I will keep you posted on the evolution of my career and I look forward to meeting you again in the future.
Best regards,
(Your name) ».

3- Never leave a meeting without getting the name of someone else to meet:
« Do you think of anyone else that you believe I should meet with for career advice? ».

4- Keep a list of all the people you meet (and their business cards) and the dates of your meetings.

**And complete your List.**

**DO STEP 2 AND STEP 3 AT THE SAME TIME:** Build your showreel and Network.

★

## STEP 4 ★ GET AN AGENT

Once (1) you have a great showreel and (2) you have a full List of industry players to contact : send your reel to the ones who are not talent agents.

Ask them (1) what they think of your showreel and (2) if they know any talent agent you could meet with.

AND NOW, you are ready to meet with talent agents. With your showreel.
Use your List to meet with them.

And while waiting for an answer from the talent agents you have met, keep acting in « indie » and student films as well as Networking.

It is only a matter of time. If you do all these steps carefully, it will happen.

Once you have an agent, you're set.
Only your talent and seriousness about your work will come into play.

Audition, audition, audition.
Act, act, act.

# ★ ★ ★ 15 GOLDEN RULES ★ ★ ★

1- **CONFIDENCE**. Anything is possible. Some people have succeeded doing it. Believe in your dream, believe in yourself. And just do it. Determination makes the difference.

2- **DISCIPLINE. Everyday DO something for your action plan.** Even if you are sick or tired. Even if it means only looking up one minute on « imdbpro » for the name of an agent to add to your List.

3- **Study smart.** Study where the industry is. USE YOUR SCHOOL: to have access to materials (resumes, showreels) and to Network.

4- **Act, act, act.** Go to NYU and the NY Film Academy. Find out about student films. Play in them. Get filmed. Act in theatre plays, independent films, TV shows, read open calls in specialized newspapers, model.

5- **Build you resume and your showreel.**

6- **Network.** Build the List of agents you'd like to meet with. Check out « imdbpro ». Ask your teachers, students, actors, friends, writers, directors etc…if they have an agent, if they know anybody in the business who you could meet with for career advice. Everyday.

7- **Network.** Always ask for a business card. Keep it.

8- **Network.** Meet with as many people as you can in the industry. Never leave a meeting without the name of another person you could meet with.

9- **Be polite and thankful.** Always send a « Thank you email ».

10- **Follow-up** with all the people you have met. Send them your reel. Ask them if they know any talent agent.

11- **When your reel is ready, you are ready to meet with talent agents. Once an agent represent you: audition, audition, audition.**

©2010, Marc Gordon

12- **Never do drugs.** Drugs will ony ruin your career and everything else in your life. You're too smart for that.

13- **Never accept to have sex with someone using his/her supposedly power on your career to date you.** Trust your instinct: you will know when this happens to you. These people will never help you. The industry is vast enough to find serious people willing to help you because they believe in your talent. And this is a business. You are the talent. You are the future star. You have the potential power. They should be as lucky to meet you as you are to meet with them.

14- **Get a degree on the side.** You will be more relaxed going to auditions knowing that you have a back-up plan. It will also help your credibility. Matt Damon, Ben Affleck and Nathalie Portman all studied at Harvard University. Moreover, by getting a degree you may be able to get a job in the Industry and build your network. Getting a degree is only a smart addition to your resume and will help people take you seriously.

15- **Information is power:** watch films, watch films, watch films, read biographies of successful actors, read the trades.

★

★ ★ ★  **DAILY CHECKLIST: YOUR PASSPORT TO SUCCESS** ★ ★ ★

**Please find next your personalized daily action plan for 30 days.**
**Fill it everyday and after 30 days, this action plan will become a habit.**
**Do at least one action per day.**

**You will be amazed by the results in ONLY 30 DAYS !**

★

## DAY 1 ★ <u>DATE:</u>

1- **Do something for yourself like eating healthily, exercising.**
   If you did today, write it down:


2- **Study, act.**
   If you did it today, write it down:


3- **Ask your acting school or contacts about roles in independent films, student films, theatre plays. Check the open calls in specialized magazines.**
   If you did it today, write it down:


4- **Ask your acting school or contacts for samples of resumes and showreels.**
   If you did it today, write it down:


5- **Complete, update your resume and showreel.**
   If you did it today, write it down:


6- **Build your List: ask your acting school or contacts if they know any talent agent OR anyone in the business who could provide you with career advice. Look up on « imdbpro » the names of agents who represented stars before they actually became stars. Complete your List.**

| INITIAL CONTACT (teacher, friend etc..) | INDUSTRY PEOPLE WHO MAY INTRODUCE YOU TO OR WITH WHOM YOU MET | NAMES OF TALENT AGENTS TARGETED |
|---|---|---|
| | | |
| | | |
| | | |

7- Meet with industry players. Always get a business card and the name of someone else to meet with. Complete your List.

8- Follow-up. Write a « Thank you email ».

Name of the person you thanked:
Date:

9- Once your showreel is ready, contact all the people on your List and send them your reel.
**Meet with talent agents.**

Name of the person you sent your showreel to:
Date:

Name of the agent you met with:
Date:

©2010, Marc Gordon

**10- Again, follow-up. Write a Thank you email.**

Name of the person you thanked:
Date:



**NOTES – REMINDERS:**




★

# DAY 2 ★ DATE:

1- **Do something for yourself like eating healthily, exercising.**
   If you did today, write it down:


2- **Study, act.**
   If you did it today, write it down:


3- **Ask your acting school or contacts about roles in independent films, student films, theatre plays. Check the open calls in specialized magazines.**
   If you did it today, write it down:


4- **Ask your acting school or contacts for samples of resumes and showreels.**
   If you did it today, write it down:


5- **Complete, update your resume and showreel.**
   If you did it today, write it down:


6- **Build your List: ask your acting school or contacts if they know any talent agent OR anyone in the business who could provide you with career advice. Look up on « imdbpro » the names of agents who represented stars before they actually became stars. Complete your List.**

| INITIAL CONTACT (teacher, friend etc..) | INDUSTRY PEOPLE WHO MAY INTRODUCE YOU TO OR WITH WHOM YOU MET | NAMES OF TALENT AGENTS TARGETED |
|---|---|---|
| | | |
| | | |
| | | |

7- Meet with industry players. Always get a business card and the name of someone else to meet with. Complete your List.

8- Follow-up. Write a « Thank you email ».

Name of the person you thanked:
Date:

9- Once your showreel is ready, contact all the people on your List and send them your reel.
**Meet with talent agents.**

Name of the person you sent your showreel to:
Date:

Name of the agent you met with:
Date:

**10- Again, follow-up. Write a Thank you email.**

Name of the person you thanked:
Date:



**NOTES – REMINDERS:**

★

# DAY 3 ★ DATE:

1- **Do something for yourself like eating healthily, exercising.**
   If you did today, write it down:

2- **Study, act.**
   If you did it today, write it down:

3- **Ask your acting school or contacts about roles in independent films, student films, theatre plays. Check the open calls in specialized magazines.**
   If you did it today, write it down:

4- **Ask your acting school or contacts for samples of resumes and showreels.**
   If you did it today, write it down:

5- **Complete, update your resume and showreel.**
   If you did it today, write it down:

6- **Build your List: ask your acting school or contacts if they know any talent agent OR anyone in the business who could provide you with career advice. Look up on « imdbpro » the names of agents who represented stars before they actually became stars. Complete your List.**

| INITIAL CONTACT (teacher, friend etc..) | INDUSTRY PEOPLE WHO MAY INTRODUCE YOU TO OR WITH WHOM YOU MET | NAMES OF TALENT AGENTS TARGETED |
|---|---|---|
|  |  |  |
|  |  |  |
|  |  |  |

7- Meet with industry players. Always get a business card and the name of someone else to meet with. Complete your List.

8- Follow-up. Write a « Thank you email ».

Name of the person you thanked:
Date:

9- Once your showreel is ready, contact all the people on your List and send them your reel.
**Meet with talent agents.**

Name of the person you sent your showreel to:
Date:

Name of the agent you met with:
Date:

**10- Again, follow-up. Write a Thank you email.**

Name of the person you thanked:
Date:


**NOTES – REMINDERS:**




★

©2010, Marc Gordon

## DAY 4 ★ DATE:

1- **Do something for yourself like eating healthily, exercising.**
   If you did today, write it down:


2- **Study, act.**
   If you did it today, write it down:


3- **Ask your acting school or contacts about roles in independent films, student films, theatre plays. Check the open calls in specialized magazines.**
   If you did it today, write it down:


4- **Ask your acting school or contacts for samples of resumes and showreels.**
   If you did it today, write it down:


5- **Complete, update your resume and showreel.**
   If you did it today, write it down:


6- **Build your List: ask your acting school or contacts if they know any talent agent OR anyone in the business who could provide you with career advice. Look up on « imdbpro » the names of agents who represented stars before they actually became stars. Complete your List.**

| INITIAL CONTACT (teacher, friend etc..) | INDUSTRY PEOPLE WHO MAY INTRODUCE YOU TO OR WITH WHOM YOU MET | NAMES OF TALENT AGENTS TARGETED |
|---|---|---|
|  |  |  |
|  |  |  |
|  |  |  |

7- Meet with industry players. Always get a business card and the name of someone else to meet with. Complete your List.

8- Follow-up. Write a « Thank you email ».

   Name of the person you thanked:
   Date:

9- Once your showreel is ready, contact all the people on your List and send them your reel.
   **Meet with talent agents.**

   Name of the person you sent your showreel to:
   Date:

   Name of the agent you met with:
   Date:

**10- Again, follow-up. Write a Thank you email.**

Name of the person you thanked:
Date:



**NOTES – REMINDERS:**



★

# DAY 5 ★ DATE:

1- **Do something for yourself like eating healthily, exercising.**
   If you did today, write it down:


2- **Study, act.**
   If you did it today, write it down:


3- **Ask your acting school or contacts about roles in independent films, student films, theatre plays. Check the open calls in specialized magazines.**
   If you did it today, write it down:


4- **Ask your acting school or contacts for samples of resumes and showreels.**
   If you did it today, write it down:


5- **Complete, update your resume and showreel.**
   If you did it today, write it down:


6- **Build your List: ask your acting school or contacts if they know any talent agent OR anyone in the business who could provide you with career advice. Look up on « imdbpro » the names of agents who represented stars before they actually became stars. Complete your List.**

©2010, Marc Gordon

| INITIAL CONTACT (teacher, friend etc..) | INDUSTRY PEOPLE WHO MAY INTRODUCE YOU TO OR WITH WHOM YOU MET | NAMES OF TALENT AGENTS TARGETED |
|---|---|---|
|  |  |  |
|  |  |  |
|  |  |  |

7- Meet with industry players. Always get a business card and the name of someone else to meet with. Complete your List.

8- Follow-up. Write a « Thank you email ».

Name of the person you thanked:
Date:

9- Once your showreel is ready, contact all the people on your List and send them your reel.
**Meet with talent agents.**

Name of the person you sent your showreel to:
Date:

Name of the agent you met with:
Date:

©2010, Marc Gordon

**10- Again, follow-up. Write a Thank you email.**

Name of the person you thanked:
Date:


**NOTES – REMINDERS:**

★

## DAY 6 ★ DATE:

1- **Do something for yourself like eating healthily, exercising.**
   If you did today, write it down:


2- **Study, act.**
   If you did it today, write it down:


3- **Ask your acting school or contacts about roles in independent films, student films, theatre plays. Check the open calls in specialized magazines.**
   If you did it today, write it down:


4- **Ask your acting school or contacts for samples of resumes and showreels.**
   If you did it today, write it down:


5- **Complete, update your resume and showreel.**
   If you did it today, write it down:


6- **Build your List: ask your acting school or contacts if they know any talent agent OR anyone in the business who could provide you with career advice. Look up on « imdbpro » the names of agents who represented stars before they actually became stars. Complete your List.**

©2010, Marc Gordon

| INITIAL CONTACT (teacher, friend etc..) | INDUSTRY PEOPLE WHO MAY INTRODUCE YOU TO OR WITH WHOM YOU MET | NAMES OF TALENT AGENTS TARGETED |
|---|---|---|
| | | |
| | | |
| | | |

7- Meet with industry players. Always get a business card and the name of someone else to meet with. Complete your List.

8- Follow-up. Write a « Thank you email ».

Name of the person you thanked:
Date:

9- Once your showreel is ready, contact all the people on your List and send them your reel.
**Meet with talent agents.**

Name of the person you sent your showreel to:
Date:

Name of the agent you met with:
Date:

©2010, Marc Gordon

**10- Again, follow-up. Write a Thank you email.**

Name of the person you thanked:
Date:


**NOTES – REMINDERS:**

★

## DAY 7 ★  DATE:

1- **Do something for yourself like eating healthily, exercising.**
   If you did today, write it down:



2- **Study, act.**
   If you did it today, write it down:



3- **Ask your acting school or contacts about roles in independent films, student films, theatre plays. Check the open calls in specialized magazines.**
   If you did it today, write it down:



4- **Ask your acting school or contacts for samples of resumes and showreels.**
   If you did it today, write it down:



5- **Complete, update your resume and showreel.**
   If you did it today, write it down:



6- **Build your List: ask your acting school or contacts if they know any talent agent OR anyone in the business who could provide you with career advice. Look up on « imdbpro » the names of agents who represented stars before they actually became stars. Complete your List.**

| INITIAL CONTACT (teacher, friend etc..) | INDUSTRY PEOPLE WHO MAY INTRODUCE YOU TO OR WITH WHOM YOU MET | NAMES OF TALENT AGENTS TARGETED |
|---|---|---|
|  |  |  |
|  |  |  |
|  |  |  |

7- Meet with industry players. Always get a business card and the name of someone else to meet with. Complete your List.

8- Follow-up. Write a « Thank you email ».

Name of the person you thanked:
Date:

9- Once your showreel is ready, contact all the people on your List and send them your reel.
**Meet with talent agents.**

Name of the person you sent your showreel to:
Date:

Name of the agent you met with:
Date:

**10- Again, follow-up. Write a Thank you email.**

    Name of the person you thanked:
    Date:

    **NOTES – REMINDERS:**

★

## DAY 8 ★ DATE:

1- **Do something for yourself like eating healthily, exercising.**
   If you did today, write it down:


2- **Study, act.**
   If you did it today, write it down:


3- **Ask your acting school or contacts about roles in independent films, student films, theatre plays. Check the open calls in specialized magazines.**
   If you did it today, write it down:


4- **Ask your acting school or contacts for samples of resumes and showreels.**
   If you did it today, write it down:


5- **Complete, update your resume and showreel.**
   If you did it today, write it down:


6- **Build your List: ask your acting school or contacts if they know any talent agent OR anyone in the business who could provide you with career advice. Look up on « imdbpro » the names of agents who represented stars before they actually became stars. Complete your List.**

©2010, Marc Gordon

| INITIAL CONTACT (teacher, friend etc..) | INDUSTRY PEOPLE WHO MAY INTRODUCE YOU TO OR WITH WHOM YOU MET | NAMES OF TALENT AGENTS TARGETED |
|---|---|---|
|  |  |  |
|  |  |  |
|  |  |  |

7- Meet with industry players. Always get a business card and the name of someone else to meet with. Complete your List.

8- Follow-up. Write a « Thank you email ».

Name of the person you thanked:
Date:

9- Once your showreel is ready, contact all the people on your List and send them your reel.
**Meet with talent agents.**

Name of the person you sent your showreel to:
Date:

Name of the agent you met with:
Date:

**10- Again, follow-up. Write a Thank you email.**

    Name of the person you thanked:
    Date:


    **NOTES – REMINDERS:**

★

## DAY 9 ★   <u>DATE:</u>

1- **Do something for yourself like eating healthily, exercising.**
   If you did today, write it down:

2- **Study, act.**
   If you did it today, write it down:

3- **Ask your acting school or contacts about roles in independent films, student films, theatre plays. Check the open calls in specialized magazines.**
   If you did it today, write it down:

4- **Ask your acting school or contacts for samples of resumes and showreels.**
   If you did it today, write it down:

5- **Complete, update your resume and showreel.**
   If you did it today, write it down:

6- **Build your List: ask your acting school or contacts if they know any talent agent OR anyone in the business who could provide you with career advice. Look up on « imdbpro » the names of agents who represented stars before they actually became stars. Complete your List.**

©2010, Marc Gordon

| INITIAL CONTACT (teacher, friend etc..) | INDUSTRY PEOPLE WHO MAY INTRODUCE YOU TO OR WITH WHOM YOU MET | NAMES OF TALENT AGENTS TARGETED |
|---|---|---|
| | | |
| | | |
| | | |

7- Meet with industry players. Always get a business card and the name of someone else to meet with. Complete your List.

8- Follow-up. Write a « Thank you email ».

Name of the person you thanked:
Date:

9- Once your showreel is ready, contact all the people on your List and send them your reel.
**Meet with talent agents.**

Name of the person you sent your showreel to:
Date:

Name of the agent you met with:
Date:

**10- Again, follow-up. Write a Thank you email.**

Name of the person you thanked:
Date:


**NOTES – REMINDERS:**

★

## DAY 10 ★ DATE:

1- **Do something for yourself like eating healthily, exercising.**
   If you did today, write it down:


2- **Study, act.**
   If you did it today, write it down:


3- **Ask your acting school or contacts about roles in independent films, student films, theatre plays. Check the open calls in specialized magazines.**
   If you did it today, write it down:


4- **Ask your acting school or contacts for samples of resumes and showreels.**
   If you did it today, write it down:


5- **Complete, update your resume and showreel.**
   If you did it today, write it down:


6- **Build your List: ask your acting school or contacts if they know any talent agent OR anyone in the business who could provide you with career advice. Look up on « imdbpro » the names of agents who represented stars before they actually became stars. Complete your List.**

©2010, Marc Gordon

| INITIAL CONTACT (teacher, friend etc..) | INDUSTRY PEOPLE WHO MAY INTRODUCE YOU TO OR WITH WHOM YOU MET | NAMES OF TALENT AGENTS TARGETED |
|---|---|---|
|  |  |  |
|  |  |  |
|  |  |  |

7- **Meet with industry players. Always get a business card and the name of someone else to meet with. Complete your List.**

8- **Follow-up. Write a « Thank you email ».**

Name of the person you thanked:
Date:

9- **Once your showreel is ready, contact all the people on your List and send them your reel.
Meet with talent agents.**

Name of the person you sent your showreel to:
Date:

Name of the agent you met with:
Date:

©2010, Marc Gordon

**10- Again, follow-up. Write a Thank you email.**

Name of the person you thanked:
Date:


**NOTES – REMINDERS:**




★

## DAY 11 ★ DATE:

1- **Do something for yourself like eating healthily, exercising.**
   If you did today, write it down:


2- **Study, act.**
   If you did it today, write it down:


3- **Ask your acting school or contacts about roles in independent films, student films, theatre plays. Check the open calls in specialized magazines.**
   If you did it today, write it down:


4- **Ask your acting school or contacts for samples of resumes and showreels.**
   If you did it today, write it down:


5- **Complete, update your resume and showreel.**
   If you did it today, write it down:


6- **Build your List: ask your acting school or contacts if they know any talent agent OR anyone in the business who could provide you with career advice. Look up on « imdbpro » the names of agents who represented stars before they actually became stars. Complete your List.**

©2010, Marc Gordon

| INITIAL CONTACT (teacher, friend etc..) | INDUSTRY PEOPLE WHO MAY INTRODUCE YOU TO OR WITH WHOM YOU MET | NAMES OF TALENT AGENTS TARGETED |
|---|---|---|
|  |  |  |
|  |  |  |
|  |  |  |

7- Meet with industry players. Always get a business card and the name of someone else to meet with. Complete your List.

8- Follow-up. Write a « Thank you email ».

Name of the person you thanked:
Date:

9- Once your showreel is ready, contact all the people on your List and send them your reel.
**Meet with talent agents.**

Name of the person you sent your showreel to:
Date:

Name of the agent you met with:
Date:

**10- Again, follow-up. Write a Thank you email.**

    Name of the person you thanked:
    Date:


**NOTES – REMINDERS:**

★

## DAY 12 ★ DATE:

1- **Do something for yourself like eating healthily, exercising.**
   If you did today, write it down:

2- **Study, act.**
   If you did it today, write it down:

3- **Ask your acting school or contacts about roles in independent films, student films, theatre plays. Check the open calls in specialized magazines.**
   If you did it today, write it down:

4- **Ask your acting school or contacts for samples of resumes and showreels.**
   If you did it today, write it down:

5- **Complete, update your resume and showreel.**
   If you did it today, write it down:

6- **Build your List: ask your acting school or contacts if they know any talent agent OR anyone in the business who could provide you with career advice. Look up on « imdbpro » the names of agents who represented stars before they actually became stars. Complete your List.**

| INITIAL CONTACT (teacher, friend etc..) | INDUSTRY PEOPLE WHO MAY INTRODUCE YOU TO OR WITH WHOM YOU MET | NAMES OF TALENT AGENTS TARGETED |
|---|---|---|
| | | |
| | | |
| | | |

7- Meet with industry players. Always get a business card and the name of someone else to meet with. Complete your List.

8- Follow-up. Write a « Thank you email ».

Name of the person you thanked:
Date:

9- Once your showreel is ready, contact all the people on your List and send them your reel.
**Meet with talent agents.**

Name of the person you sent your showreel to:
Date:

Name of the agent you met with:
Date:

**10- Again, follow-up. Write a Thank you email.**

Name of the person you thanked:
Date:

**NOTES – REMINDERS:**

★

## DAY 13 ★ DATE:

1- **Do something for yourself like eating healthily, exercising.**
   If you did today, write it down:


2- **Study, act.**
   If you did it today, write it down:


3- **Ask your acting school or contacts about roles in independent films, student films, theatre plays. Check the open calls in specialized magazines.**
   If you did it today, write it down:


4- **Ask your acting school or contacts for samples of resumes and showreels.**
   If you did it today, write it down:


5- **Complete, update your resume and showreel.**
   If you did it today, write it down:


6- **Build your List: ask your acting school or contacts if they know any talent agent OR anyone in the business who could provide you with career advice. Look up on « imdbpro » the names of agents who represented stars before they actually became stars. Complete your List.**

©2010, Marc Gordon

| INITIAL CONTACT (teacher, friend etc..) | INDUSTRY PEOPLE WHO MAY INTRODUCE YOU TO OR WITH WHOM YOU MET | NAMES OF TALENT AGENTS TARGETED |
|---|---|---|
|  |  |  |
|  |  |  |
|  |  |  |

7- Meet with industry players. Always get a business card and the name of someone else to meet with. Complete your List.

8- Follow-up. Write a « Thank you email ».

Name of the person you thanked:
Date:

9- Once your showreel is ready, contact all the people on your List and send them your reel.
**Meet with talent agents.**

Name of the person you sent your showreel to:
Date:

Name of the agent you met with:
Date:

©2010, Marc Gordon

**10- Again, follow-up. Write a Thank you email.**

Name of the person you thanked:
Date:


**NOTES – REMINDERS:**

★

## DAY 14 ★ DATE:

1- **Do something for yourself like eating healthily, exercising.**
   If you did today, write it down:


2- **Study, act.**
   If you did it today, write it down:


3- **Ask your acting school or contacts about roles in independent films, student films, theatre plays. Check the open calls in specialized magazines.**
   If you did it today, write it down:


4- **Ask your acting school or contacts for samples of resumes and showreels.**
   If you did it today, write it down:


5- **Complete, update your resume and showreel.**
   If you did it today, write it down:


6- **Build your List: ask your acting school or contacts if they know any talent agent OR anyone in the business who could provide you with career advice. Look up on « imdbpro » the names of agents who represented stars before they actually became stars. Complete your List.**

©2010, Marc Gordon

| INITIAL CONTACT (teacher, friend etc..) | INDUSTRY PEOPLE WHO MAY INTRODUCE YOU TO OR WITH WHOM YOU MET | NAMES OF TALENT AGENTS TARGETED |
|---|---|---|
|  |  |  |
|  |  |  |
|  |  |  |

7- Meet with industry players. Always get a business card and the name of someone else to meet with. Complete your List.

8- Follow-up. Write a « Thank you email ».

Name of the person you thanked:
Date:

9- Once your showreel is ready, contact all the people on your List and send them your reel.
**Meet with talent agents.**

Name of the person you sent your showreel to:
Date:

Name of the agent you met with:
Date:

**10- Again, follow-up. Write a Thank you email.**

Name of the person you thanked:
Date:

**NOTES – REMINDERS:**

★

## DAY 15 ★ DATE:

1- **Do something for yourself like eating healthily, exercising.**
   If you did today, write it down:


2- **Study, act.**
   If you did it today, write it down:


3- **Ask your acting school or contacts about roles in independent films, student films, theatre plays. Check the open calls in specialized magazines.**
   If you did it today, write it down:


4- **Ask your acting school or contacts for samples of resumes and showreels.**
   If you did it today, write it down:


5- **Complete, update your resume and showreel.**
   If you did it today, write it down:


6- **Build your List: ask your acting school or contacts if they know any talent agent OR anyone in the business who could provide you with career advice. Look up on « imdbpro » the names of agents who represented stars before they actually became stars. Complete your List.**

©2010, Marc Gordon

| INITIAL CONTACT (teacher, friend etc..) | INDUSTRY PEOPLE WHO MAY INTRODUCE YOU TO OR WITH WHOM YOU MET | NAMES OF TALENT AGENTS TARGETED |
|---|---|---|
|  |  |  |
|  |  |  |
|  |  |  |

7- Meet with industry players. Always get a business card and the name of someone else to meet with. Complete your List.

8- Follow-up. Write a « Thank you email ».

Name of the person you thanked:
Date:

9- Once your showreel is ready, contact all the people on your List and send them your reel.
**Meet with talent agents.**

Name of the person you sent your showreel to:
Date:

Name of the agent you met with:
Date:

©2010, Marc Gordon

**10- Again, follow-up. Write a Thank you email.**

Name of the person you thanked:
Date:

**NOTES – REMINDERS:**

★

## DAY 16 ★ DATE:

1- **Do something for yourself like eating healthily, exercising.**
   If you did today, write it down:

2- **Study, act.**
   If you did it today, write it down:

3- **Ask your acting school or contacts about roles in independent films, student films, theatre plays. Check the open calls in specialized magazines.**
   If you did it today, write it down:

4- **Ask your acting school or contacts for samples of resumes and showreels.**
   If you did it today, write it down:

5- **Complete, update your resume and showreel.**
   If you did it today, write it down:

6- **Build your List: ask your acting school or contacts if they know any talent agent OR anyone in the business who could provide you with career advice. Look up on « imdbpro » the names of agents who represented stars before they actually became stars. Complete your List.**

©2010, Marc Gordon

| INITIAL CONTACT (teacher, friend etc..) | INDUSTRY PEOPLE WHO MAY INTRODUCE YOU TO OR WITH WHOM YOU MET | NAMES OF TALENT AGENTS TARGETED |
|---|---|---|
| | | |
| | | |
| | | |

7- Meet with industry players. Always get a business card and the name of someone else to meet with. Complete your List.

8- Follow-up. Write a « Thank you email ».

Name of the person you thanked:
Date:

9- Once your showreel is ready, contact all the people on your List and send them your reel.
**Meet with talent agents.**

Name of the person you sent your showreel to:
Date:

Name of the agent you met with:
Date:

**10- Again, follow-up. Write a Thank you email.**

Name of the person you thanked:
Date:

**NOTES – REMINDERS:**

★

## DAY 17 ★ DATE:

1- **Do something for yourself like eating healthily, exercising.**
   If you did today, write it down:


2- **Study, act.**
   If you did it today, write it down:


3- **Ask your acting school or contacts about roles in independent films, student films, theatre plays. Check the open calls in specialized magazines.**
   If you did it today, write it down:


4- **Ask your acting school or contacts for samples of resumes and showreels.**
   If you did it today, write it down:


5- **Complete, update your resume and showreel.**
   If you did it today, write it down:


6- **Build your List: ask your acting school or contacts if they know any talent agent OR anyone in the business who could provide you with career advice. Look up on « imdbpro » the names of agents who represented stars before they actually became stars. Complete your List.**

| INITIAL CONTACT (teacher, friend etc..) | INDUSTRY PEOPLE WHO MAY INTRODUCE YOU TO OR WITH WHOM YOU MET | NAMES OF TALENT AGENTS TARGETED |
|---|---|---|
| | | |
| | | |
| | | |

7- **Meet with industry players. Always get a business card and the name of someone else to meet with. Complete your List.**

8- **Follow-up. Write a « Thank you email ».**

Name of the person you thanked:
Date:

9- **Once your showreel is ready, contact all the people on your List and send them your reel.**
**Meet with talent agents.**

Name of the person you sent your showreel to:
Date:

Name of the agent you met with:
Date:

©2010, Marc Gordon

**10- Again, follow-up. Write a Thank you email.**

Name of the person you thanked:
Date:

**NOTES – REMINDERS:**

★

## DAY 18 ★ DATE:

1- **Do something for yourself like eating healthily, exercising.**
   If you did today, write it down:

2- **Study, act.**
   If you did it today, write it down:

3- **Ask your acting school or contacts about roles in independent films, student films, theatre plays. Check the open calls in specialized magazines.**
   If you did it today, write it down:

4- **Ask your acting school or contacts for samples of resumes and showreels.**
   If you did it today, write it down:

5- **Complete, update your resume and showreel.**
   If you did it today, write it down:

6- **Build your List: ask your acting school or contacts if they know any talent agent OR anyone in the business who could provide you with career advice. Look up on « imdbpro » the names of agents who represented stars before they actually became stars. Complete your List.**

©2010, Marc Gordon

| INITIAL CONTACT (teacher, friend etc..) | INDUSTRY PEOPLE WHO MAY INTRODUCE YOU TO OR WITH WHOM YOU MET | NAMES OF TALENT AGENTS TARGETED |
|---|---|---|
| | | |
| | | |
| | | |

7- **Meet with industry players. Always get a business card and the name of someone else to meet with. Complete your List.**


8- **Follow-up. Write a « Thank you email ».**

Name of the person you thanked:
Date:


9- **Once your showreel is ready, contact all the people on your List and send them your reel.
Meet with talent agents.**

Name of the person you sent your showreel to:
Date:

Name of the agent you met with:
Date:

©2010, Marc Gordon

**10- Again, follow-up. Write a Thank you email.**

Name of the person you thanked:
Date:

**NOTES – REMINDERS:**

★

## DAY 19 ★ DATE:

1- **Do something for yourself like eating healthily, exercising.**
   If you did today, write it down:


2- **Study, act.**
   If you did it today, write it down:


3- **Ask your acting school or contacts about roles in independent films, student films, theatre plays. Check the open calls in specialized magazines.**
   If you did it today, write it down:


4- **Ask your acting school or contacts for samples of resumes and showreels.**
   If you did it today, write it down:


5- **Complete, update your resume and showreel.**
   If you did it today, write it down:


6- **Build your List: ask your acting school or contacts if they know any talent agent OR anyone in the business who could provide you with career advice. Look up on « imdbpro » the names of agents who represented stars before they actually became stars. Complete your List.**

©2010, Marc Gordon

| INITIAL CONTACT (teacher, friend etc..) | INDUSTRY PEOPLE WHO MAY INTRODUCE YOU TO OR WITH WHOM YOU MET | NAMES OF TALENT AGENTS TARGETED |
|---|---|---|
| | | |
| | | |
| | | |

7- **Meet with industry players. Always get a business card and the name of someone else to meet with. Complete your List.**

8- **Follow-up. Write a « Thank you email ».**

   Name of the person you thanked:
   Date:

9- **Once your showreel is ready, contact all the people on your List and send them your reel.**
   **Meet with talent agents.**

   Name of the person you sent your showreel to:
   Date:

   Name of the agent you met with:
   Date:

©2010, Marc Gordon

**10- Again, follow-up. Write a Thank you email.**

    Name of the person you thanked:
    Date:


**NOTES – REMINDERS:**

★

## DAY 20 ★ DATE:

1- **Do something for yourself like eating healthily, exercising.**
   If you did today, write it down:


2- **Study, act.**
   If you did it today, write it down:


3- **Ask your acting school or contacts about roles in independent films, student films, theatre plays. Check the open calls in specialized magazines.**
   If you did it today, write it down:


4- **Ask your acting school or contacts for samples of resumes and showreels.**
   If you did it today, write it down:


5- **Complete, update your resume and showreel.**
   If you did it today, write it down:


6- **Build your List: ask your acting school or contacts if they know any talent agent OR anyone in the business who could provide you with career advice. Look up on « imdbpro » the names of agents who represented stars before they actually became stars. Complete your List.**

| INITIAL CONTACT (teacher, friend etc..) | INDUSTRY PEOPLE WHO MAY INTRODUCE YOU TO OR WITH WHOM YOU MET | NAMES OF TALENT AGENTS TARGETED |
|---|---|---|
| | | |
| | | |
| | | |

7- Meet with industry players. Always get a business card and the name of someone else to meet with. Complete your List.

8- Follow-up. Write a « Thank you email ».

Name of the person you thanked:
Date:

9- Once your showreel is ready, contact all the people on your List and send them your reel.
**Meet with talent agents.**

Name of the person you sent your showreel to:
Date:

Name of the agent you met with:
Date:

**10- Again, follow-up. Write a Thank you email.**

Name of the person you thanked:
Date:


**NOTES – REMINDERS:**




★

## DAY 21 ★ DATE:

1- **Do something for yourself like eating healthily, exercising.**
   If you did today, write it down:

2- **Study, act.**
   If you did it today, write it down:

3- **Ask your acting school or contacts about roles in independent films, student films, theatre plays. Check the open calls in specialized magazines.**
   If you did it today, write it down:

4- **Ask your acting school or contacts for samples of resumes and showreels.**
   If you did it today, write it down:

5- **Complete, update your resume and showreel.**
   If you did it today, write it down:

6- **Build your List: ask your acting school or contacts if they know any talent agent OR anyone in the business who could provide you with career advice. Look up on « imdbpro » the names of agents who represented stars before they actually became stars. Complete your List.**

| INITIAL CONTACT (teacher, friend etc..) | INDUSTRY PEOPLE WHO MAY INTRODUCE YOU TO OR WITH WHOM YOU MET | NAMES OF TALENT AGENTS TARGETED |
|---|---|---|
| | | |
| | | |
| | | |

7- Meet with industry players. Always get a business card and the name of someone else to meet with. Complete your List.

8- Follow-up. Write a « Thank you email ».

Name of the person you thanked:
Date:

9- Once your showreel is ready, contact all the people on your List and send them your reel.
**Meet with talent agents.**

Name of the person you sent your showreel to:
Date:

Name of the agent you met with:
Date:

**10- Again, follow-up. Write a Thank you email.**

    Name of the person you thanked:
    Date:


**NOTES – REMINDERS:**

★

## DAY 22 ★   <u>DATE:</u>

1- **Do something for yourself like eating healthily, exercising.**
   If you did today, write it down:


2- **Study, act.**
   If you did it today, write it down:


3- **Ask your acting school or contacts about roles in independent films, student films, theatre plays. Check the open calls in specialized magazines.**
   If you did it today, write it down:


4- **Ask your acting school or contacts for samples of resumes and showreels.**
   If you did it today, write it down:


5- **Complete, update your resume and showreel.**
   If you did it today, write it down:


6- **Build your List: ask your acting school or contacts if they know any talent agent OR anyone in the business who could provide you with career advice. Look up on « imdbpro » the names of agents who represented stars before they actually became stars. Complete your List.**

| INITIAL CONTACT (teacher, friend etc..) | INDUSTRY PEOPLE WHO MAY INTRODUCE YOU TO OR WITH WHOM YOU MET | NAMES OF TALENT AGENTS TARGETED |
|---|---|---|
| | | |
| | | |
| | | |

7- **Meet with industry players. Always get a business card and the name of someone else to meet with. Complete your List.**

8- **Follow-up. Write a « Thank you email ».**

Name of the person you thanked:
Date:

9- **Once your showreel is ready, contact all the people on your List and send them your reel.
Meet with talent agents.**

Name of the person you sent your showreel to:
Date:

Name of the agent you met with:
Date:

**10- Again, follow-up. Write a Thank you email.**

Name of the person you thanked:
Date:


**NOTES – REMINDERS:**




★

## DAY 23 ★ DATE:

**1- Do something for yourself like eating healthily, exercising.**
If you did today, write it down:


**2- Study, act.**
If you did it today, write it down:


**3- Ask your acting school or contacts about roles in independent films, student films, theatre plays. Check the open calls in specialized magazines.**
If you did it today, write it down:


**4- Ask your acting school or contacts for samples of resumes and showreels.**
If you did it today, write it down:


**5- Complete, update your resume and showreel.**
If you did it today, write it down:


**6- Build your List: ask your acting school or contacts if they know any talent agent OR anyone in the business who could provide you with career advice. Look up on « imdbpro » the names of agents who represented stars before they actually became stars. Complete your List.**

©2010, Marc Gordon

| INITIAL CONTACT (teacher, friend etc..) | INDUSTRY PEOPLE WHO MAY INTRODUCE YOU TO OR WITH WHOM YOU MET | NAMES OF TALENT AGENTS TARGETED |
|---|---|---|
| | | |
| | | |
| | | |

7- **Meet with industry players. Always get a business card and the name of someone else to meet with. Complete your List.**


8- **Follow-up. Write a « Thank you email ».**

Name of the person you thanked:
Date:


9- **Once your showreel is ready, contact all the people on your List and send them your reel.**
**Meet with talent agents.**

Name of the person you sent your showreel to:
Date:

Name of the agent you met with:
Date:

**10- Again, follow-up. Write a Thank you email.**

Name of the person you thanked:
Date:

**NOTES – REMINDERS:**

★

## DAY 24 ★ DATE:

1- **Do something for yourself like eating healthily, exercising.**
   If you did today, write it down:


2- **Study, act.**
   If you did it today, write it down:


3- **Ask your acting school or contacts about roles in independent films, student films, theatre plays. Check the open calls in specialized magazines.**
   If you did it today, write it down:


4- **Ask your acting school or contacts for samples of resumes and showreels.**
   If you did it today, write it down:


5- **Complete, update your resume and showreel.**
   If you did it today, write it down:


6- **Build your List: ask your acting school or contacts if they know any talent agent OR anyone in the business who could provide you with career advice. Look up on « imdbpro » the names of agents who represented stars before they actually became stars. Complete your List.**

| INITIAL CONTACT (teacher, friend etc..) | INDUSTRY PEOPLE WHO MAY INTRODUCE YOU TO OR WITH WHOM YOU MET | NAMES OF TALENT AGENTS TARGETED |
|---|---|---|
|  |  |  |
|  |  |  |
|  |  |  |

7- Meet with industry players. Always get a business card and the name of someone else to meet with. Complete your List.

8- Follow-up. Write a « Thank you email ».

Name of the person you thanked:
Date:

9- Once your showreel is ready, contact all the people on your List and send them your reel.
**Meet with talent agents.**

Name of the person you sent your showreel to:
Date:

Name of the agent you met with:
Date:

**10- Again, follow-up. Write a Thank you email.**

Name of the person you thanked:
Date:

**NOTES – REMINDERS:**

★

## DAY 25 ★ DATE:

1- **Do something for yourself like eating healthily, exercising.**
   If you did today, write it down:


2- **Study, act.**
   If you did it today, write it down:


3- **Ask your acting school or contacts about roles in independent films, student films, theatre plays. Check the open calls in specialized magazines.**
   If you did it today, write it down:


4- **Ask your acting school or contacts for samples of resumes and showreels.**
   If you did it today, write it down:


5- **Complete, update your resume and showreel.**
   If you did it today, write it down:


6- **Build your List: ask your acting school or contacts if they know any talent agent OR anyone in the business who could provide you with career advice. Look up on « imdbpro » the names of agents who represented stars before they actually became stars. Complete your List.**

| INITIAL CONTACT (teacher, friend etc..) | INDUSTRY PEOPLE WHO MAY INTRODUCE YOU TO OR WITH WHOM YOU MET | NAMES OF TALENT AGENTS TARGETED |
|---|---|---|
|  |  |  |
|  |  |  |
|  |  |  |

7- **Meet with industry players. Always get a business card and the name of someone else to meet with. Complete your List.**

8- **Follow-up. Write a « Thank you email ».**

   Name of the person you thanked:
   Date:

9- **Once your showreel is ready, contact all the people on your List and send them your reel.**
   **Meet with talent agents.**

   Name of the person you sent your showreel to:
   Date:

   Name of the agent you met with:
   Date:

**10- Again, follow-up. Write a Thank you email.**

Name of the person you thanked:
Date:

**NOTES – REMINDERS:**

★

## DAY 26 ★ DATE:

1- **Do something for yourself like eating healthily, exercising.**
   If you did today, write it down:


2- **Study, act.**
   If you did it today, write it down:


3- **Ask your acting school or contacts about roles in independent films, student films, theatre plays. Check the open calls in specialized magazines.**
   If you did it today, write it down:


4- **Ask your acting school or contacts for samples of resumes and showreels.**
   If you did it today, write it down:


5- **Complete, update your resume and showreel.**
   If you did it today, write it down:


6- **Build your List: ask your acting school or contacts if they know any talent agent OR anyone in the business who could provide you with career advice. Look up on « imdbpro » the names of agents who represented stars before they actually became stars. Complete your List.**

©2010, Marc Gordon

| INITIAL CONTACT (teacher, friend etc..) | INDUSTRY PEOPLE WHO MAY INTRODUCE YOU TO OR WITH WHOM YOU MET | NAMES OF TALENT AGENTS TARGETED |
|---|---|---|
|  |  |  |
|  |  |  |
|  |  |  |

7- Meet with industry players. Always get a business card and the name of someone else to meet with. Complete your List.

8- Follow-up. Write a « Thank you email ».

Name of the person you thanked:
Date:

9- Once your showreel is ready, contact all the people on your List and send them your reel.
**Meet with talent agents.**

Name of the person you sent your showreel to:
Date:

Name of the agent you met with:
Date:

**10- Again, follow-up. Write a Thank you email.**

Name of the person you thanked:
Date:


**NOTES – REMINDERS:**

★

**DAY 27 ★ DATE:**

1- **Do something for yourself like eating healthily, exercising.**
   If you did today, write it down:


2- **Study, act.**
   If you did it today, write it down:


3- **Ask your acting school or contacts about roles in independent films, student films, theatre plays. Check the open calls in specialized magazines.**
   If you did it today, write it down:


4- **Ask your acting school or contacts for samples of resumes and showreels.**
   If you did it today, write it down:


5- **Complete, update your resume and showreel.**
   If you did it today, write it down:


6- **Build your List: ask your acting school or contacts if they know any talent agent OR anyone in the business who could provide you with career advice. Look up on « imdbpro » the names of agents who represented stars before they actually became stars. Complete your List.**

©2010, Marc Gordon

| INITIAL CONTACT (teacher, friend etc..) | INDUSTRY PEOPLE WHO MAY INTRODUCE YOU TO OR WITH WHOM YOU MET | NAMES OF TALENT AGENTS TARGETED |
|---|---|---|
| | | |
| | | |
| | | |

7- **Meet with industry players. Always get a business card and the name of someone else to meet with. Complete your List.**

8- **Follow-up. Write a « Thank you email ».**

Name of the person you thanked:
Date:

9- **Once your showreel is ready, contact all the people on your List and send them your reel.
Meet with talent agents.**

Name of the person you sent your showreel to:
Date:

Name of the agent you met with:
Date:

**10- Again, follow-up. Write a Thank you email.**

Name of the person you thanked:
Date:


**NOTES – REMINDERS:**

★

## DAY 28 ★ DATE:

1- **Do something for yourself like eating healthily, exercising.**
   If you did today, write it down:


2- **Study, act.**
   If you did it today, write it down:


3- **Ask your acting school or contacts about roles in independent films, student films, theatre plays. Check the open calls in specialized magazines.**
   If you did it today, write it down:


4- **Ask your acting school or contacts for samples of resumes and showreels.**
   If you did it today, write it down:


5- **Complete, update your resume and showreel.**
   If you did it today, write it down:


6- **Build your List: ask your acting school or contacts if they know any talent agent OR anyone in the business who could provide you with career advice. Look up on « imdbpro » the names of agents who represented stars before they actually became stars. Complete your List.**

| INITIAL CONTACT (teacher, friend etc..) | INDUSTRY PEOPLE WHO MAY INTRODUCE YOU TO OR WITH WHOM YOU MET | NAMES OF TALENT AGENTS TARGETED |
|---|---|---|
| | | |
| | | |
| | | |

7- Meet with industry players. Always get a business card and the name of someone else to meet with. Complete your List.

8- Follow-up. Write a « Thank you email ».

Name of the person you thanked:
Date:

9- Once your showreel is ready, contact all the people on your List and send them your reel.
**Meet with talent agents.**

Name of the person you sent your showreel to:
Date:

Name of the agent you met with:
Date:

©2010, Marc Gordon

**10- Again, follow-up. Write a Thank you email.**

Name of the person you thanked:
Date:

**NOTES – REMINDERS:**

★

## DAY 29 ★ DATE:

1- **Do something for yourself like eating healthily, exercising.**
   If you did today, write it down:


2- **Study, act.**
   If you did it today, write it down:


3- **Ask your acting school or contacts about roles in independent films, student films, theatre plays. Check the open calls in specialized magazines.**
   If you did it today, write it down:


4- **Ask your acting school or contacts for samples of resumes and showreels.**
   If you did it today, write it down:


5- **Complete, update your resume and showreel.**
   If you did it today, write it down:


6- **Build your List: ask your acting school or contacts if they know any talent agent OR anyone in the business who could provide you with career advice. Look up on « imdbpro » the names of agents who represented stars before they actually became stars. Complete your List.**

| INITIAL CONTACT (teacher, friend etc..) | INDUSTRY PEOPLE WHO MAY INTRODUCE YOU TO OR WITH WHOM YOU MET | NAMES OF TALENT AGENTS TARGETED |
|---|---|---|
| | | |
| | | |
| | | |

7- **Meet with industry players. Always get a business card and the name of someone else to meet with. Complete your List.**


8- **Follow-up. Write a « Thank you email ».**

Name of the person you thanked:
Date:


9- **Once your showreel is ready, contact all the people on your List and send them your reel.**
**Meet with talent agents.**

Name of the person you sent your showreel to:
Date:

Name of the agent you met with:
Date:

**10- Again, follow-up. Write a Thank you email.**

Name of the person you thanked:
Date:


**NOTES – REMINDERS:**


★

## DAY 30 ★ DATE:

1- **Do something for yourself like eating healthily, exercising.**
   If you did today, write it down:


2- **Study, act.**
   If you did it today, write it down:


3- **Ask your acting school or contacts about roles in independent films, student films, theatre plays. Check the open calls in specialized magazines.**
   If you did it today, write it down:


4- **Ask your acting school or contacts for samples of resumes and showreels.**
   If you did it today, write it down:


5- **Complete, update your resume and showreel.**
   If you did it today, write it down:


6- **Build your List: ask your acting school or contacts if they know any talent agent OR anyone in the business who could provide you with career advice. Look up on « imdbpro » the names of agents who represented stars before they actually became stars. Complete your List.**

| INITIAL CONTACT (teacher, friend etc..) | INDUSTRY PEOPLE WHO MAY INTRODUCE YOU TO OR WITH WHOM YOU MET | NAMES OF TALENT AGENTS TARGETED |
|---|---|---|
|  |  |  |
|  |  |  |
|  |  |  |

7- Meet with industry players. Always get a business card and the name of someone else to meet with. Complete your List.

8- Follow-up. Write a « Thank you email ».

Name of the person you thanked:
Date:

9- Once your showreel is ready, contact all the people on your List and send them your reel.
**Meet with talent agents.**

Name of the person you sent your showreel to:
Date:

Name of the agent you met with:
Date:

**10- Again, follow-up. Write a Thank you email.**

Name of the person you thanked:
Date:

**NOTES – REMINDERS:**

★

Made in the USA  
Columbia, SC  
12 January 2018